(**TITLE PAGE**) *Graceful and effortless in flight* *the snowy egret visits the lower Colorado River* *each winter. Common in marsh grass backwater* *at Imperial National Wildlife Refuge, some have* *become "regulars" at sites like Martinez Lake.* PETER ENSENBERGER

Motion illustrations CARLTONS' PHOTOGRAPHI

Arizona
Wild & Free
Text by Stewart L. Udall
with Randy Udall

ARIZONA
HIGHWAYS BOOK
In cooperation with
Arizona Game and Fish Department

Photographs by Arizona Highways Contributors

Forest Lands

Rising from the desert floor to 8,000 feet above sea level, the Mogollon Rim is painted by the warm glow of sunset. At various heights, this great escarpment stretches across more than 200 miles of Arizona and into New Mexico as the Mogollon Mountains. The Rim's conifer forest is home to numerous wildlife species. Look carefully and you'll see a partially hidden elk.
RICK ODELL

Scrub and Grasslands

Found throughout Arizona, mule deer live in the cool high country as well as the blistering Sonoran Desert. The two varieties, Rocky Mountain and the smaller Desert mule deer, are named for their mule-like ears. Here Rocky Mountain does forage in the scrub and grassland.
JACK DYKINGA

Desert Lands

Fifteen years ago Arizona had fewer than a dozen known bald eagle breeding areas. Today there are 31. Primarily fish eaters, they commonly build their nests in tall trees near lakes or streams. Cliff-nesting, pictured here, is unique to Arizona.

ROGER WEBER

Wet Lands

Although classified as nocturnal, the raccoon is often active in the morning and evening and, occasionally, at midday.
With its black face mask and roly-poly body, this easily identified carnivore lives close to water and feeds on fish,
crayfish, birds, eggs, fruit, and vegetables. This family portrait likely captures a mother and her two offspring.
ROBERT CAMPBELL

Prepared by the Book Division of *Arizona Highways* magazine, a monthly publication of the Arizona Department of
Transportation. Hugh Harelson — Publisher / Wesley Holden — Managing Editor / Melanie Johnston — Text Editor
Peter Ensenberger — Picture Editor / Gary Bennett — Creative Director / Cindy Mackey — Production Manager
Vicky Snow — Production Assistant.

Library of Congress Catalog Number 93-70887   ISBN 0-916179-41-9

1
0

Sheltered in shade, young cottontail rabbits use their siblings for pillows. Cottontails inhabit the entire
state and reproduce rapidly. Several species reside in Arizona. Most prominent among them are the
Western (sometimes called mountain cottontail), the Desert, and even the Eastern.
JERRY JACKA

Contents

1

Prologue

In 1930, the summer I turned 10, one of my uncles developed an obsession, as devout fishermen sometimes do. The object was *Salmo apache*, the Apache trout that can be found in only a few small streams in the White Mountains of northeastern Arizona. Scouting around, talking to old-timers and ranchers who knew the country, he came up with a list of streams that were said to harbor "natives," as we called them. Whenever he invited me to accompany him on his quest, I'd jump at the chance since fishing beat farming any day.

Typically, we'd leave our homes in the small hamlet of St. Johns before dawn each Saturday. We'd drive the highway to Springerville, then turn onto a rutted road that plowed through the ponderosas. After a bit, we'd branch off onto a logging track. When that gave out, we'd grab our poles and hike through the forest to little high-country streams. Then the best fishing I've ever experienced would begin.

Those creeks were rarely more than 10 feet wide. The beautiful speckled trout were similarly small. Twelve inches was considered a lunker. The water was clear as gin and cold as icemelt, fresh from the snowbanks that huddled in the shade. If the light was behind you as you stalked upstream, you could often see the fish hiding below a big rock or fallen log. Seeing them was one thing, catching them another. They were easily spooked. The slightest movement

or strange shadow would send them fleeing for a hiding place.

The creeks dwindled as we climbed. By 10,500 feet they were mere rivulets a yard or two wide. The trout had shrunk too, but still they swam, facing upstream, as if finning to heaven. Late in the afternoon, if my creel was empty, I'd grow frustrated. Sometimes I'd wade into the creek, groping under cutbanks, trying to bear-paw a trout out. On other days, I'd forget about fishing to explore the grassy meadows through which these creeks meandered. Dappled with wildflowers and tall grasses, they had a sweet fragrance. It was the smell of a natural, pristine world, and it evoked feelings I had never felt before.

I did not know it then, but those trips were a watershed for me. There, in my tenth year, in those alpine glades below the wind-whipped summit of Mt. Baldy, I discovered what was for me the headwaters of Arizona's wild and free environment. This was the beginning of my lifelong love affair with Nature.

1
3

(LEFT) *With polychromatic feathers shifting colors and with flaps down, a mallard drake brakes for a water landing. This abundant duck has even been seen paddling in irrigation ditches within Phoenix city limits. Its Mexican cousin, which also inhabits Arizona, wears darker plumage.*
JAMES TALLON

(FOLLOWING PANEL, PAGES 14-15)
At the southern boundary of the Fort Apache Indian Reservation, the Black River tumbles toward its junction with the Salt River. Along with rainbow and secretive brown trout, the feisty smallmouth bass swims here. The Black River is highly rated by anglers who favor remote regions.
LARRY ULRICH

A R I Z O N A

Wild

by

Stewart L.
Udall

I once saw a billboard alongside a high-way outside Williams that made a lasting impression on me. Erected by a real estate agent, the sign proclaimed in bright red letters: "*Remember! Only 17% of Arizona can be bought and sold!*"

"Thank God," I laughed, and drove on. Later, pondering the sales pitch, I realized it encapsulated one of Arizona's great advantages. It's true that only 17 percent of the state is private land. The remaining 83 percent, about 60 million acres, is held in trust for us all. The federal government owns half; Indian reservations account for one-third; and the state manages the rest. Much of this land, a surprising amount, remains natural and untrammeled.

As of 1992, 4.4 million acres of the public domain had been legally designated as wilderness. But must a place be designated "wilderness" to be wild and free? Of course not. Wilderness areas are drawn with lines on a map. Wildness, conversely, can't be corralled between arbitrary boundaries. It is deeper, more primal, more intrinsic. Wildness is within. And not just within the land. As the poet Gary Snyder puts it, there is a bobcat in the forest and one in the mind.

By my estimate, at least one-fourth and perhaps as much as one-half of Arizona's public domain, 15 to 30 million acres — the larger figure equalling an area the size of Maine — remains free in spirit and wild in character. Don't accept my word for this. See for

& Free

yourself. Get in your car and drive away from the city. As the sub-
urbs and shopping malls fall behind, Nature laps up to the highway,
quietly reasserting control.

Hike up one of the canyons that tumble into Tucson. Within an
hour you will be in remote, rough country. From 17,000-acre
South Mountain Park, in Phoenix, there are wild niches from
which you can see Central Avenue skyscrapers. A few minutes'
walk from downtown Prescott or Flagstaff are expansive forests
into which one can easily disappear. Despite the influx of people
and the inroads of progress this century has seen, across much of
Arizona, the land's authentic pulse remains wild and free.

After World War II, I moved to Tucson to attend the
University of Arizona. When I arrived, the city still had some of
the rudiments of a 19th-century outpost. Within the city limits
were large, unbroken tracts of creosote, the saguaro-clad foothills
were largely undeveloped, and the populace had struck an easy
truce with its surroundings.

My wife, Lee, and I married in 1947; our first son was born a
year later. The outdoors became an integral part of our family life.
When our children (eventually there would be six) were little, we
took them to Sabino Canyon, where they frolicked in the pools of
that enchanting stream, and to Mt. Lemmon, where we introduced

(OPPOSITE PAGE) *A praying mantis, one of the food chain's most effective predators, waits for a meal to wander within range of its powerful mandibles.*
GEORGE H. H. HUEY

them to ponderosa pines and snow. These were beginnings, preludes. As our two eldest sons grew stronger, we began taking hikes together. It was on one of these outings that they first glimpsed Arizona's wild visage.

After entering Bear Canyon, we had been forced to wade the channel countless times. Our tennis shoes were spongy, squelching with each step. The drainage narrowed, steepened. The sandy bottom surrendered to rock, the sun to shade. As we clambered higher beside sculpted pools, the walls pinched in. A moist breath of wind came down-canyon, carrying with it an aura of mystery, potential. Rounding a bend, we heard a clatter on rock. Then another. Searching for the disturbance, we spied four bighorn sheep high on the wall. A full-curl ram peered down at us in that dispassionate, now-I've-seen-it-all way that old sheep affect. The boys gaped back, quivering in excitement. Such moments never last long. The ram and his flock nimbly traversed the cliff face and disappeared from view. But not from memory. From that day forward, my boys possessed a mental image of wild America.

In 1955, when I was elected to Congress, we moved to Washington, D.C. But each summer we made it a point to return west for an outdoor adventure. One year we ran the Grand Canyon on rafts. Another year we took a jeep-and-hiking tour of the slickrock canyons on the Colorado Plateau. Exploring secret canyons, singing around the campfire, sleeping under the stars — these journeys were precious interludes.

Supposedly "on vacation," the kids sometimes learned more than they did in school; this was, for them, a second education. They learned how to read a topo map and the importance of a good canteen. They learned that cottonwoods meant water and that a mile by foot is different from one by car. They learned to give cholla cactus a wide berth — and how to remove its spines from their shins when they didn't. They learned how to bake a birthday cake in a Dutch oven. They learned that August's thick, drumming rain-storms could, through persistence, give birth to spectacular flash floods. Mostly, though, the kids learned about themselves, about self-reliance. And, though we rarely discussed it in so many words, about the beauty and grandeur of Nature's world.

Early in this century, Santa Fe author Mary Austin wrote of the Southwest, "I . . . annex to my own estate a very great territory to which none has surer title." This is what all of us should try to do. Annex parcels of this great territory to ourselves. Pledge allegiance to it. Get to know the land and the messages it whispers to those willing to listen.

Here's my tried-and-true recipe for annexing a mountain: Take your kids. Your spouse. A friend. Go climb it. Sleep on the top. You are there just for a day and a night. Nothing is bought. Nothing is sold. But by your labors you have purchased something of inestimable value. Forever after you will scan that peak from far off and know it as a friend, know its smell and textures. You've annexed it. It has become part of your life experience.

Climbing a mountain, running a river, exploring a canyon — these phrases connote arduous journeys. Indeed it would be hard, if not impossible, to annex some of the remote places portrayed on these pages without breaking a sweat. But annexing the wild and free does not have to be a gut-wrenching, perspiration-soaked endeavor. It can, instead, be an artistic, intellectual, spiritual exercise. The tools don't have to be a pair of hiking boots, a backpack, kayak, or climbing rope. They can be binoculars, easel, sketchbook, field guide, fishing rod, camera, or just the emulsion of the mind. I'll share an example from my own experience.

This day I will always remember. After scrutinizing maps and anything else I could find on the subject, I concluded that in the summer of 1540 Coronado and his conquistadors must have crossed

1
9

the Black River near Big Bonita Creek. And now, as our party reaches the end of a boulder-choked road, the gradual slope of the ridge across the river hints that this is the place we seek. My anticipation grows as we wade the river. I can scarcely suppress my excitement, exclaiming, "We may be approaching a natural trail that leads up to the Natanes Plateau and the meadow where Coronado pitched a camp. If so, in a few minutes we will be walking on what doubtless is the oldest identifiable non-Indian historic trail in the United States!" (It is worth noting that if, by some miracle of reincarnation, Coronado were to reappear in Arizona today, he would have no trouble orienting himself. After 450 years, more than 80 percent of the corridor the conquistadores followed through Arizona remains wild country unmarred by cities or surfaced roads.)

How should you begin your own entrada into the wild and free? If you are a newcomer, you might start by visiting some of Arizona's dozens of state and national parks, monuments, recreation areas, and wildlife refuges. If you enjoy what you find, branch out. Some of the best journeys have been launched by curiosity and a map: What would you see from the top of Granite Mountain? What's a good winter hike in the Kofa National Wildlife Refuge? Would it be possible to go up that canyon, cross that divide, and come out here?

You can also begin your hike in a library. Bookshelves make wonderful trailheads. Bone up on human and natural history, geology, and so forth. Peruse back issues of *Arizona Highways* magazine. Let this research and your other interests shape your journeys. The possibilities are endless. If, for example, your passion is botany, you might see how many of the rare plants found on the Mohave Desert you can photograph. A bird-watcher might arrange a rendezvous in Patagonia with hummingbirds fresh from the jungles of Central America. I don't subscribe to the belief

that there's gold cached in the Superstitions, but it would be intriguing to search for some of the abandoned turquoise mines the Anasazi worked or the silver mines mentioned by Father Francisco Eusebio Kino. If you believe, as many do, that the wild and free has a spiritual dimension, you might attempt to read its runes, decipher its mysteries, and translate its ineffable scriptures.

On the strength of my experience, I'm convinced that anyone can discover a rewarding path into the wild and free. Age and physical condition matter less than attitude. Sure, some things probably should be left to teenagers, but being gray-haired forecloses less than we sometimes think.

W hat's out there to discover?

Beauty. First and foremost. On every scale, from the minuscule to the majestic, Arizona is replete with scenic grandeur. Awe inspiring, haunting, serene, alluring — every imaginable flavor of beauty is there. Like a kaleidoscope, Arizona's natural panorama constantly shifts with the seasons, the weather, the light.

By immersing yourself in this state's unspoiled country, you can also experience one of the world's last great reservoirs of spaciousness and solitude. Despite the population boom of recent decades, Arizona remains sparsely settled. I recall reading an interview with an Italian visitor who said, "You are very lucky to live here. We are so crowded we dream of open space." As it happens, Italy and Arizona are about the same size. But where Arizona has 3.6 million people, or about 32 per square mile, Italy has 57 million, or 500 per square mile.

Arizona's spacious wild areas are a precious legacy. The original landscapes of Europe and those of the eastern United States have vanished under a sea of humanity. Arizona has 92 wilderness areas; New York has one. In all of New England there are only eight. With space comes solitude, a rare resource that is getting rarer still.

(OPPOSITE PAGE) *Often colloquialized as a "horny toad," this harmless reptile is properly recognized as the "horned lizard." Its suit of armor effectively turns aside the thorns of the prickly pear cactus.*
PAUL A. BERQUIST

2
1

Thankfully, there are many places in Arizona where one can escape the grinding racket of civilization, the clangor and din, to be utterly alone. "There is something about living in big empty space," Wallace Stegner once wrote, "where people are few and distant, under a great sky . . . that not only tells an individual how small he is, but steadily tells him who he is."

This squares with my boyhood memories of St. Johns. From the time we were five years old our world was as big as our legs could carry us during a long day. Finding a coyote den or a nest of eagles — we had adventures Huckleberry Finn would have envied. In such a spacious, reflective environment there were also priceless opportunities for us to get a sense of ourselves while we were developing a feel for the earth. An appreciation of the beauty and wonder of life is hard to teach in a classroom. We learned ours out in the open in a duckblind, waiting for flights of mallards to arrive, or watching thunderstorms march across the horizon.

Arizona's remote reaches also had a profound influence on the naturalist Aldo Leopold, who worked as a forest ranger in the White Mountains during the second decade of this century, and later, in his classic book, *Sand County Almanac*, wrote feelingly of the "high solitude" and "aristocracy of space" he discovered there.

When Leopold first arrived in Arizona, he was, by his own admission, "young and full of trigger-itch." As was the wont in those days, he rarely passed up a chance to gun down a predator. After watching the slow death of a wolf he had shot, Leopold began to have second thoughts. Soon he was trying to "think like a mountain," to understand the "hidden meaning in the howl of the wolf, long known among mountains, but seldom perceived among men." In his later years, Leopold would wonder "who wrote the rules for progress," as he became the nation's most eloquent proponent of the then-radical concept of treating land not as a commodity belonging to us but as a community to which we belong.

2
2

(OPPOSITE PAGE) *Only the sharpest-eyed can correctly sort out Arizona's many hummingbird species. The male Costa's sports a distinctive metallic purple cap and whisker-like feathers on its throat.*
C. ALLAN MORGAN

As Leopold seems to have recognized, Arizona isn't just a stronghold for scenery and wildlife, it is also a spiritual retreat with the power to bring humans into harmony with the natural world. Today, more than ever, we need places where young and old alike can forge a bond with the earth. For us as individuals and for our species, learning what the wild and free has to teach is no trivial pursuit; increasingly, it seems to be a matter of survival. As writer David Rains Wallace puts it, "Civilization no longer needs to open up wilderness; it needs wilderness to help open up the still largely unexplored human mind."

Nature, in her blind search for life, has filled every possible cranny ... with some sort of fantastic creature.
— Joseph Wood Krutch

What is it exactly that makes Arizona a special place? I would argue that it's the stunning variety of climates, scenery, and wildlife. Arizona is much more than the sum of its parts. It has a natural dynamic, a synergy matched by few other places. Arizona is another planet, or more precisely, another topography. Everything I love about this state is rooted in the landscape.

It is often said that Arizona is a land of extremes, of expansive deserts and lofty mountains and so on. And it is. But our state is unique not because it boasts both mountains and deserts — this is true of many regions — but because its mountains and deserts are so jumbled together. Standing on the street in the desert metropolis of Tucson one can see three mountain ranges whose summits approach or exceed 9,000 feet. Between Tucson (elevation 2,600 feet) and nearby Mt. Wrightson (9,453 feet), there is more vertical relief than can be found between any two similar points east of the Mississippi. And Wrightson is more than 3,000 feet lower than

12,643-foot Humphreys Peak, Arizona's tallest.

Throw a ruler on a map of Arizona. Draw a line between two distant cities almost anywhere. Imagine hiking from Phoenix to Show Low, Flagstaff to Prescott, or Tucson to Douglas. You'll discover a topsy-turvy, tortured landscape as rough and corrugated as a washboard, a place chockful of canyons and calderas, mountains and mesas, buttes and bajadas, glades and gullies, chasms and crags.

Because Arizona is so rich in natural nooks and crannies, it has a corresponding wealth of "fantastic creatures." This treasure trove can be measured in many coins. For example, 16 eastern states share one species of chipmunk; Arizona has five. The East — the whole thing, from Florida to Maine, from Illinois to Virginia — has two skunk species. A single mountain in Arizona is home to four. Birds? Five hundred species have been spotted in the state. Butterflies? Three hundred species.

Arizona's unspoiled country is an ecological frontier. This is where North meets South, East meets West, hot meets cold, wet meets dry; a place where black bears live cheek by jowl with Gila monsters; where a hiker can risk sunstroke one day and hypothermia the next. Considered in isolation (as they tend to be), these juxtapositions are easily dismissed as freakish, biotic believe-it-or-nots. Collectively, however, they suggest that Arizona's ecological possibilities are wilder and more extravagant than most people can imagine. To experience this, climb one of the mountains that tower above our southern deserts. It is a hike I made some years ago.

As dawn breaks, the summit looms high overhead. You eat quickly and start up. By 9 o'clock you are 1,500 feet off the desert floor and have left the creosote and paloverde behind. Gradually, spiny plants yield to leafy ones. By 10 A.M. you've passed the uppermost saguaro. (Its location marks an invisible isotherm; these cactus can't tolerate more than 36 hours of frost.) By noon you're hot and tired, sitting in the shade of an oak, eating lunch 3,000 feet higher than you did breakfast. A short siesta and then it's up again. Two hours later, as the trail cuts through a sheltered draw, you take another break, this time on a bed of pine needles under a ponderosa. Tree by tree, the forest builds. At 4 P.M. you reach a spring. Ferns abound and there are mule deer tracks in the mud. Next you encounter an Engelmann spruce, its sharp scent a welcome tonic. Clouds build and it starts to rain. Within minutes you are soaked and shivering. As you totter up the last few steps to the summit, your legs feel as if you've hiked from Mexico to Canada — and, in a way, you have.

On such a hike you will pass through four or five "life zones," a concept first promulgated a century ago by the eminent scientist C. Hart Merriam, who did his seminal work in and around the Grand Canyon. Since Merriam's day many of America's finest ecologists have come to Arizona to study the Santa Rita, Catalina, Galiuro, Pinaleno, Chiricahua, and Huachuca mountain ranges. Each of these airy arks is a world in miniature, a natural laboratory

(OPPOSITE PAGE) *Found throughout Arizona, gregarious mourning doves prefer to congregate in large flocks in the southern part of the state, particularly near fields of grain.*
INGE MARTIN

harboring its own unique assemblage of rare plants and animals.

Like the tundra plants on the San Francisco Peaks and Apache trout in the White Mountains, many of these species are Ice Age flotsam, organisms stranded in high places like so many bottles on a beach. But not all "Pleistocene relicts" are found in mountain environments; some of the most critically endangered species are restricted to desert or scrubland, creatures such as the Ramsey Canyon leopard frog, which is found along just one small stream coming out of the Huachuca Mountains.

(OPPOSITE PAGE) *Drawn by the fragrance of a Rocky Mountain iris, this Western tiger swallowtail butterfly, one of numerous species hosted in Arizona, drops by to siphon nectar.* EDWARD McCAIN

The variety and beauty of the natural world can best be preserved only if man feels the necessity of sharing the earth with at least some of his fellow creatures to be a privilege rather than an irritation.

—Joseph Wood Krutch

What does the future hold for the 5,000 species of plants and animals that share the wild and free? While the majority are in good shape, about 10 percent of Arizona's biota, roughly 500 species, are threatened with extinction. Many of these species are now "prisoners of geography," confined to small "islands" of habitat. This is cause for concern, because when plants or animals are confined to a restricted habitat they become more vulnerable to extinction. Life for them is a crapshoot. Lately mankind has loaded the dice.

Over the last 100 years, our actions have begun to erode our natural heritage. But rather than lament what's lost, I suggest we redouble our efforts to preserve what's left. To protect what remains of the wild and free we humans must become more sensitive to the needs of other species and more ingenious at adapting our activities to Arizona's unique environment. We may never be able to match the kangaroo rat's ability to metabolize water from its food, but we can learn to use natural resources more efficiently than we do today.

It's time to begin, in Aldo Leopold's words, "thinking like a mountain." Whether the "crop" our public lands provide is sawlogs, grass, or recreational user-days, the objective should be to harvest a sustainable yield without further damaging the wildlife habitat. If we manage the public domain wisely and protect our remaining natural rivers, then Arizona's treasure trove of plants and animals will survive as a "biological inheritance" for future generations. Today, environmental organizations such as The Nature Conservancy are working valiantly to protect critical natural habitats. And never before have so many Arizonans, young and old, become actively involved in wildlife conservation.

While much work remains, much has already been accomplished. Arizonans should be proud of their conservation heritage. Today, our state has more wilderness areas than any other. It can boast the only major city in the nation, Tucson, that is bordered on three sides by a wilderness estate within walking distance of its inhabitants. Some of the streams I fished as a young boy are safely enveloped in the Mt. Baldy Wilderness Area — preserved for my grandchildren and yours.

In the years to come, let's all take that pejorative term "landgrabber" and give it a new twist. Let us go out onto the land, not to possess it but to savor it, not to git-and-run but to grow and relish, not to grab with our hands but to caress with our minds. Take your family, your friends, and go. Sit at the foot of a ponderosa. Wade in a stream. Sleep on the ground. Smell the desert rain. Experience the mystique of open spaces, the glory of Arizona, wild and free.

Pure wildness is the one great present want.
—John Muir

Carrying a centipede lunch, possibly to be shared with its brood, this burrowing owl checks for threats before entering the lair.
These long-legged, small owls commonly nest in abandoned rodent burrows, thus their name.
C. ALLAN MORGAN

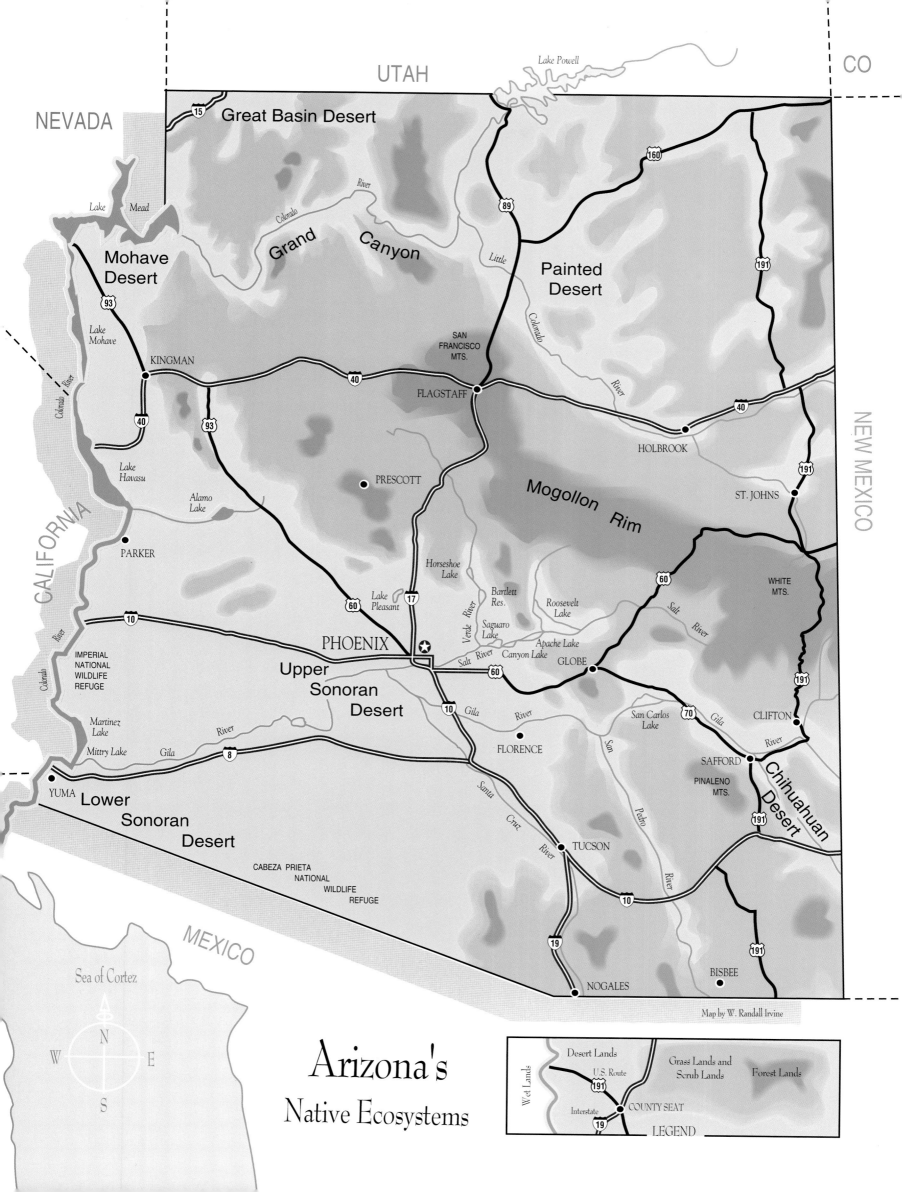

Arizona's
Native Ecosystems

Map by W. Randall Irvine

LEGEND

Desert Lands | Grass Lands and Scrub Lands | Forest Lands

Wet Lands

U.S. Route — 191

Interstate — 19

COUNTY SEAT

Forest

Rattling through the aspens, whirling leaves into the evening sky, the autumn storm races into the Kachina Peaks Wilderness Area. Icy raindrops slant down as my companion and I hasten to pitch a tent. Guylines taut, we crawl inside to warm our frozen fingers. Sometime after midnight, I awake. Poking my head out, I discover that the rain has turned to snow.

By morning the front has moved on, leaving an exquisite mosaic of golden leaves atop the fresh-fallen blanket of white. After a long summer in Phoenix, the frosty scene seems miraculous. Fumbling with matches, I light a stove to boil water for tea and oatmeal. Breakfast over, we start hiking. We've got an appointment — not with the great peak looming overhead — but with a rare tree that grows high on its shoulders.

In a few miles, the now-slushy trail departs the shimmering aspens and enters an alpine forest of fir and spruce. Another hour and we break free into a sunlit meadow where the pass above stands in bold relief. After crossing it and contouring onto the rocky south-facing slope beyond, we encounter a grove of contorted pines, their branches extending at awkward angles like pennants in a stiff breeze. Is this what we've come to see? I consult a field guide. Short needles, five to the bundle, branchlets resemble foxtails — yes! these are bristlecone pines, the oldest living trees on the planet.

I've read much about these trees but never before seen one. On Great Basin mountaintops, bristlecones may live to be 4,800 years old — although the oldest one found here on Humphreys Peak (the

Lands

only place in Arizona they grow) is a comparatively youthful 1,446 years. Bristlecones sometimes reach 60 feet in height, but most of the gnarled specimens on this exposed site are less than 30 feet tall. Dropping my daypack, I survey this grove of amazing trees.

Unlike other species of evergreens whose members often resemble one another, each of these trees is a distinctive individual, pruned by wind, sculpted by time. Here and there, weathered-gray snags lie heaped up like driftwood on a beach. Their massive trunks flayed of bark, these trees look dead, but not all are: Some still send forth green branches in homage to the sun. These ancient arboreal monarchs have a tenacious wildness within, a primal presence that is humbling. I find myself wishing I could speak to them.

(LEFT) *Whether perched on a conifer tree or a saguaro cactus, the red-tailed hawk is equally at home in the open desert or the plush forest. During mating season, it soars and wheels in the thermals while calling a distinctive "keeeeer."*
JAMES TALLON

Somewhere in the high, clean silences on this mountain is a tree that first took root two centuries after the birth of Christ. Others were old when nearby Sunset Crater spit fire in 1065. They hark back to a time when Betatakin, Chaco Canyon, and Mesa Verde were the great cities of the Southwest. If old bristlecones are a window into the past, young ones are a lifeline to the future. This sapling beside me now today may live to see the year 3000.

Why should the longest-lived trees be found 11,000 feet above sea level in one of the earth's harshest climates? This is a great riddle. In Europe biologists call the area around timberline the *kampf-zone,* or "zone of struggle." It's an apt term. Fierce blizzards, battering winds, ultraviolet radiation, avalanches, lightning — bristlecones endure all of these. But how? What's their secret? Some scientists suggest that the species' hardiness, its ability to take root in thin soils and survive killing temperatures of 30 below zero, gives it a competitive advantage over frailer organisms. In this view, the bristlecone achieves its astounding longevity by triumphing over extraordinary adversity. Is there a lesson here?

My speculations are cut short by a chilling gust of wind. It's time to go down. But first, I take a last look around. The U.S. Forest Service manages nearly 11 million acres of Arizona, and this lofty perch commands an unsurpassed view of what I like to think of as "our forests." To the northwest, the green bulge of the Kaibab Plateau breaks the horizon. To the southeast, the world's largest stand of ponderosa pine rolls unbroken along the Mogollon Rim for more than 150 miles to New Mexico. Out of sight in that direction lies Escudilla, the blue-domed mountain that bound my boyhood. Farther south, the ponderosas reappear, along with spruce, cypress, and Apache pine, on the so-called "sky islands" of the Sonoran Desert — the Santa Rita, Catalina, Galiuro, Pinaleno, Chiricahua, and Huachuca mountain ranges. Trees, trees, trees — so many varieties of trees in a state better known for its cactus.

As we take our leave of the bristlecones and start down the talus, I reflect that we are all rich in being free to explore these forests and climb these peaks, gain their glad tidings, and, for a brief hour, "annex" them to our personal estate.

(OPPOSITE PAGE) *On a ridge of the San Francisco Peaks, time and unrelenting wind and weather have sculpted this bristlecone pine into arresting art. Bristlecones may be the oldest trees on Earth. Some on San Francisco Peaks are more than 1400 years old.*
DAVID MUENCH

3
2

(FOLLOWING PANEL, PAGES 34-35) *An October storm, a harbinger of winter, deep snows, and solitude, rolls across the Coconino National Forest blanketing the upper reaches of Oak Creek Canyon. The Cococino represents a large portion of the largest expanse of ponderosa pines in the world.*
LES MANEVITZ

(LEFT) *Playing the mating game, eight male Abert squirrels pursue a lone female up a snag. Some researchers say this ritual takes place just one day a year. The tassel-eared Abert is intrinsically linked to the ponderosa pine tree. The squirrel buries caches of cones in the forest floor, but forgets where some of them are hidden. The lost cones germinate into trees.* JAMES TALLON

3 7

(ABOVE) *Although a healthy population of mountain lions endures in Arizona, the animal's reclusive disposition and the remote regions it inhabits make spotting one a rare treat. Sometimes called a "cougar," it feeds primarily on deer. Like most predators, it favors lookouts that allow expansive views of its territory.* KEVIN K. HARRIS

(FOLLOWING PANEL, PAGES 38-39) *Dwarfed by the 12,643-foot-high San Francisco Peaks, a group of elk leisurely munches meadow grass. By 1897 Arizona's native Merriam elk had been hunted into extinction. However, a program that transplanted the very similar Rocky Mountain elk from Yellowstone National Park, between 1913 and 1928, has produced a current population of more than 40,000 of the high-country inhabitants.* BILL GOBUS

(RIGHT) *After an August rain, umbrella-shaped mushrooms spring from a log in the Santa Catalina Mountains*
RANDY A. PRENTICE

(ABOVE) *Heat warms reptilian blood, allowing the quick movements of this short-horned lizard, sunning itself on Kaibab fungi. Once it achieves the "right temperature," it scours the forest floor for its favorite foods—ants, spiders, and other insects.*
JAMES TALLON

(FOLLOWING PANEL, PAGES 42-43) *An estimated 2,500 of the rarely sighted, solitary black bears inhabit Arizona's forest and scrub lands. Often parodied as a campground scavenger that routs picnickers while looking for fast food, the black bear can be dangerous. It depends largely on a diet of grubs, berries, acorns, small rodents, carrion, and the occasional fruit of the prickly pear cactus.*
KEVIN K. HARRIS

4
1

42

(LEFT) *Though classed as nocturnal, the porcupine can sometimes be seen in the daytime shuffling along the forest floor or hunched into a ball in a tree. It has a fondness for the inner bark of pine trees, sometimes girdling trees and killing them. If the forest floor is littered with a collection of twigs stripped of their bark, called "salad sticks," it is a sign that a porcupine has dined at the top of a nearby tree. The guard hairs of Western porcupines are yellowish, giving their coats a sun-bleached appearance.*
BRUCE TUCKER

4
5

(ABOVE) *An apartment-hunting striped skunk will favor natural cavities, like those found in felled trees. Maligned for its odor, the skunk discharges its musk in defense only. Arizona claims four species of skunks: spotted, striped, hooded, and hognosed.*
JOHN CANCALOSI

(RIGHT) *Sneezeweed and oxeye daisy dominate this White Mountain meadow, providing uprights where spiders can tie their silken traps. Among the numerous species of flowers found in surrounding highlands are those with familiar names, such as penstemon, Indian paintbrush, lupine, goldenrod, coneflower, and columbine.*
LARRY ULRICH

(ABOVE) *Strutting across Hannagan Meadow in the White Mountains, Merriam's turkey hens and poults hunt for seeds and insects. Though its weight sometimes exceeds 20 pounds, the wild turkey is an excellent flyer. It roosts in trees, but prefers to make its escape on the ground. In the quiet of the wilderness, the gobble of the male can be heard more than a mile away. The turkey is considered one of the wariest animals in the wild.*
P.K. WEIS

(FOLLOWING PANEL, PAGES **48-49**)
In the Apache-Sitgreaves National Forest, a Rocky Mountain mule deer doe raises her head in curiosity. Spruce and fir trees are indicators of high elevation — this region is about 9,000 feet above sea level. Mule deer does and fawns are rarely alone; others probably forage just inside the forest's edge.
JACK DYKINGA

(**LEFT**) *Contrary to its off-putting name, the banks along Deadman Creek, on Mt. Graham in the Pinaleno Mountains, are alive with lush mountain flora.*
JACK DYKINGA

5
1

(**ABOVE**) *Most often called "ladybugs," another common name for this tiny beetle is "ladybird." This one has alighted on a branch of Western bracken. In May and June millions of ladybugs blanket Arizona's forested high country.*
D.W. LAZAROFF

(**FOLLOWING PANEL, PAGES 52-53**) *This volcanic cinder cone, covered with grass and wildflowers, rises island-like out of the surrounding forest near Flagstaff. Rather than germinate all at once, wildflowers, like these on Government Knolls, emerge over several weeks, thus minimizing chances of their extinction in the wake of a freeze.*
TOM BEAN

Normally secretive, preferring the cover of trees and brush, these white-tailed deer are a momentary exception to the rule. The Coues deer that range along the Arizona-Mexico border are a smaller edition of the white-tailed. Both are easily distinguishable from mule deer by their large "white flag" tails, buck antler tines that branch from a single beam, and a smooth-running rather than bounding gait.
PAUL A. BERQUIST

5
4

(ABOVE) *In a mountain meadow, a bull elk guards its harem from any amorous intrusion by outsiders. The second largest member of the deer family, bull elk weigh 600 to 1,100 pounds. The tip of prime antlers may be 8 or 9 feet off the ground.*
FRANK ZULLO

55

5
7

(RIGHT) *Sunrise at Hawley Lake attracts trout-hungry anglers. This conifer-fringed 260-acre lake, created by the White Mountain Apache Tribe, is a cornerstone of the White Mountain Recreation Area.*
DAVID MUENCH

(ABOVE) *A mule deer doe pauses before entering the forest. Besides meadow grasses, mule deer feed on cliffrose, mushrooms, mistletoe, and, above 8,000 feet, the bark of quaking aspen trees.*
DEBS METZONG

5
9

Scrub and
Grass

I stand on a ruin gazing out at the grassy valley below. It is February and the snowcapped summits in the distance shimmer hypnotically as I imagine the life of the Indians who lived here long ago. A call breaks my reverie: "Here, come look at this."

On the far side of an earthen mound, a friend I regard as an Arizona treasure stoops over and plucks a potsherd from the ground. He is Dr. Emil Haury, the dean of Southwestern archaeologists. For 50 years Emil has searched for "Red House" — a fabled way station where Coronado rested his horses in 1540 during that most important of European *entradas* into the greater Southwest. On this Sunday I have joined Emil to search the lush lower slopes of the Pinaleno Mountains near Bonita, Arizona. Dreams of unearthing a knife, spur, or any metal artifact from Coronado's expedition that would pinpoint the exact location of the Red House are dashed, but the exploration is exhilarating nonetheless.

Lying between mountain and desert, Arizona's scrublands and grasslands are worlds unto themselves, worlds full of potential, places where even the most distant horizon seems within reach. I remember the free-as-the-wind feeling I experienced as a boy while riding horseback across piñon and juniper-dotted prairies near my home. Later in life, I came to relish the grass-clad Arizona Strip north of the Grand Canyon and the rugged chaparral that lies westward from Prescott to the Colorado River. To this day, whenever I

Lands

venture out onto a grassland, part of me intuitively feels as if I'm coming home.

The relationship between *Homo sapiens* and grass is ancient. Fossil evidence suggests that an African savanna was our birthplace. From archaeological digs we know that men and women have roamed the grassy valleys of southern Arizona for more than 11,000 years.

On my day with Emil, I was struck again by the transforming power of this sun-washed, windswept realm. As one's senses are reborn, worldly cares and thoughts of past and future fall away, leaving the immediate present — the breeze in one's face, the hawk soaring overhead, the swaying blades of grama grass underfoot.

Walt Whitman never saw the West, nor imbibed its spacious grandeur, but these lines of his capture the spirit that Arizona's grasslands evoke:

I inhale great draughts of space.

The east and west are mine,

and the north and south are mine.

I am larger, better than I thought,

I did not know I held so much goodness.

6
1

(LEFT) *At full tilt, this mule deer doe departs a grassy meadow for the sanctuary of a nearby stand of piñon and juniper scrub.*
JAMES TALLON

(FOLLOWING PANEL, PAGES 62-63)
Across much of Arizona, July and August mornings are cloudless, yet by midafternoon, lightning dashes across the skies, thunder vibrates the earth, and rain refreshes the thirsty grasslands. This summer storm is building over Williamson Valley near Prescott.
CHRISTINE KEITH

(BELOW) *Incorrectly called "antelope," the pronghorn is unique to*
North America. In Arizona it inhabits grassy plains, where it can
best use its main defense: speed. It has been clocked at more than 60
miles per hour.
JAMES TALLON

6
6

(**LEFT**) *Peeping through a stand of weeds, a coyote pauses while catching grasshoppers. Not highly selective, the coyote includes birds, rodents, carrion, and an occasional domestic animal in its diet. In the past, the coyote has been subjected to one of the greatest mass animal poisonings ever instituted by humans. Now that their incredible ability to control rodents is widely recognized, coyotes are more welcome.*
JAMES TALLON

6
7

(**ABOVE**) *Widespread in scrub and grassland, the black-tailed jackrabbit rates second in speed only to the pronghorn. When pursued it can cover ground in 15-foot bounds. Six-foot-high leaps allow it to spot its pursuer and correct its escape route. The antelope jackrabbit found in lower Arizona grasslands, like those at Oracle Junction, has even longer ears. In both types, their enormous ears, networked with blood-vessels, are more than sound-gathering devices: They serve as cooling radiators.*
PAUL A. BERQUIST

(**FOLLOWING PANEL, PAGES 68-69**) *The agave is also called the century plant because it takes so long to bloom. A member of the lily family, the agave may actually take up to 25 years to bloom, depending on where it is growing. When its 12- to 18-foot flowering stalk blooms, the agave dies. Native Americans found multiple uses for the agave, making food, drink, fiber, soap, and medicine from its roots and broad leaves.*
RANDY A. PRENTICE

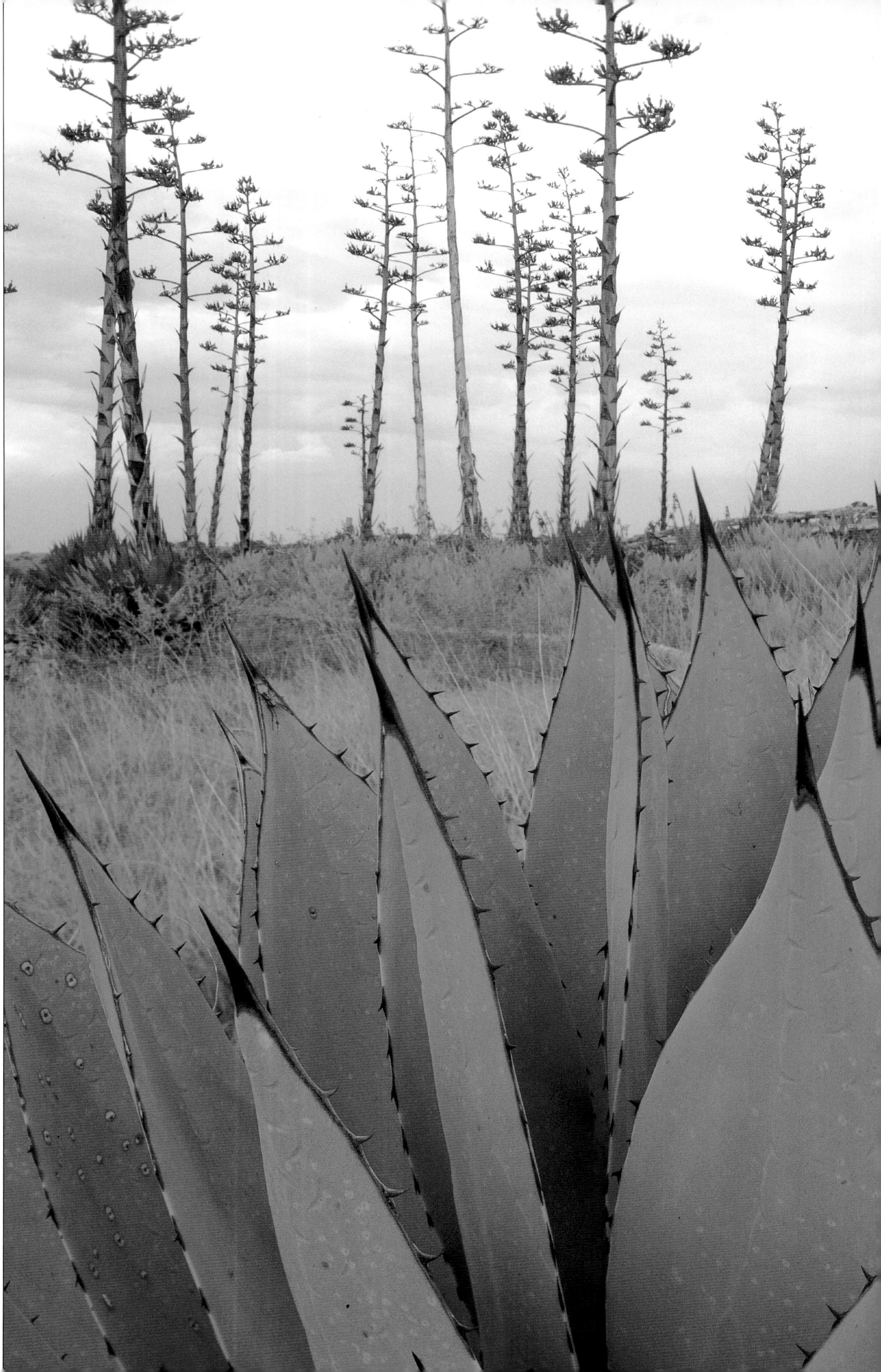

7
1

*Arizona is visited by as many as 15 species
of hummingbirds. Ramsey Canyon in
southeastern Arizona has gained national
attention as a magnet for flocks of
bird-watchers.*
CHARLES S. RAU

(ABOVE) *Isolated by the camera, this coyote has siblings and parents within yelping range. Among the most caring of wildlife parents, coyotes have been observed sacrificing their lives to save those of their pups. As an adult, this pup could weigh as much as 30 pounds.*
BERNADETTE M. HEATH

(FOLLOWING PANEL, PAGES 74-75) *One of Nature's staples of life, for humans as well as animals, is the red fruit of the prickly pear cactus. Prickly pear grows over a wide range of elevations from the forest to scrubland to the low desert. It is a favorite of javelinas, which ignore the do-not-touch spines and eat the cactus — fruit, pad, spines, and all.*
JOHN DREW

74

76

(LEFT) *Just an inch under 2 feet long, the roadrunner ranks as the largest of the American cuckoos. It does indeed run roads, preferring the unpaved, and sometimes paces cars at speeds up to 15 miles per hour. Its diet consists of insects, rodents, small birds, lizards, and snakes. A daring snake killer, the roadrunner is able to avoid the lightning-like strikes of rattlers.*
PAUL A. BERQUIST

7 7

(ABOVE) *Perched on a boulder, a golden-mantled ground squirrel chews on a grassy tidbit. Unlike chipmunks, it has no stripes on the sides of its face. In Arizona it inhabits scrub and conifer forests, living in burrows and hibernating in winter.*
INGE MARTIN

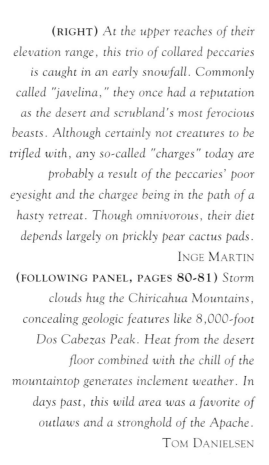

(RIGHT) *At the upper reaches of their elevation range, this trio of collared peccaries is caught in an early snowfall. Commonly called "javelina," they once had a reputation as the desert and scrubland's most ferocious beasts. Although certainly not creatures to be trifled with, any so-called "charges" today are probably a result of the peccaries' poor eyesight and the chargee being in the path of a hasty retreat. Though omnivorous, their diet depends largely on prickly pear cactus pads.*
INGE MARTIN

(FOLLOWING PANEL, PAGES 80-81) *Storm clouds hug the Chiricahua Mountains, concealing geologic features like 8,000-foot Dos Cabezas Peak. Heat from the desert floor combined with the chill of the mountaintop generates inclement weather. In days past, this wild area was a favorite of outlaws and a stronghold of the Apache.*
TOM DANIELSEN

(ABOVE) *Montezuma quail have been identified by several names, but are customarily called Mearn's quail in Arizona. Although the birds once were thought to be extinct in the state, a group of hunter-conservationists, sans shotguns and using pointing dogs, scoured the birds' bunchgrass habitat near Patagonia and discovered hundreds of them. Simply put, one must almost step on this species to inspire flight.*

CHARLES S. RAU

(BELOW) *In contrast to Montezuma quail, the scaled quail spooks easily. It prefers to make its get-away on foot through the habitat of grass, brush, and scrub. With blue-gray breast feathers rimmed in black, the scaled quail does have a "scaley" look.*

CHARLES S. RAU

Though less wary than the mountain lion, the bobcat is rarely seen by other than determined
outdoor folk. Equally at home in the desert, scrub, or forest, it prefers to prowl its terrain at
night. Like a housecat, the bobcat sometimes kills for "fun" rather than for food.
CHARLES S. RAU

Desert

"It will be dark soon. Let's find a place to sleep."

Photographer Jerry Jacka steers the four-wheel-drive Suburban off the dusty track we've been following into an arroyo. Tonight we can disregard the rule that says "never camp in a dry wash," for it is February and we are in the Cabeza Prieta National Wildlife Refuge, by Nature's command one of the most arid and lonely reaches of the state.

As the sun slips toward the horizon, the temperature plummets. Jerry and I don sweaters, then kindle a small fire — the only kind possible in a place where some years it never rains and a green leaf is always an extravagance. We cook a can of baked beans and a skillet of hamburger, a simple meal that seems in harmony with the sparseness of our desert surroundings. Dinner over, we let the fire burn down to coals. Resting nearby in our sleeping bags, we lie back to watch a star show.

The Milky Way stretches across the inky void like a neon belt. Orion stands high in the southern sky. No man-made light or sound disrupts this sublime display, and we realize that it has been 48 hours since we last saw another human being. Indeed, bounded on the north by the 130-mile-long U.S. Air Force Gunnery Range and on the south by Mexico's desolate Gran Desierto, this is one of the most alone places in America.

Jerry and I are retracing a journey made almost 300 years before by Father Francisco Eusebio Kino, one of the first Europeans to

Lands

explore this wild outback. Now, as the heavens wheel overhead, we find ourselves marveling at the unwavering faith that guided the Jesuit priest on his explorations. What sustained him as he traveled over 7,500 miles on foot and horseback during the seven-year period between 1694 and 1701? What gave him the strength to venture out time and again into one of the driest deserts in North America, where water can be found only in widely scattered *tinajas* or natural tanks, like the one we had visited earlier in the day?

There are no certain answers to such questions. But in my life I have always found wilderness to be a wellspring of inspiration. Indeed, to my way of thinking, many of Arizona's wild places are "outdoor cathedrals," with the power to invigorate our souls. From my studies of Kino's life, I long ago concluded that he drew spiritual sustenance from the vastness through which he rode, much of which remains little changed today.

But this evening, as the constellations dance overhead, I gain a deeper understanding of this man. I had always pictured the padre on horse-

Weighing up to 15 pounds, stretching to more than seven feet long, and being short-tempered makes the Western diamondback rattlesnake a deadly adversary. Contrary to common belief, the snake does not always rattle before striking, and the age cannot be determined by its number of rattles (some may break off after molting).
CHARLES S. RAU

back, sweltering in the daytime heat — never huddled around a meager fire on a cold winter night. This was a serious omission on my part. The reason: Kino's journeys into the desert heartland were all made between October and the end of March, when cool temperatures enable horses to travel long distances without water. But days are short in winter — darkness rules more than the sun. That being the case, Kino must have spent hundreds of nights shivering under a saddle blanket, looking at the stars above. I know that Kino was more than an idle stargazer because early in 1702 he recorded sighting a comet that passed across the constellation of Aquarius.

And so I'm left wondering: Isn't it likely that Kino took nourishment not only from the land underfoot but also from the sky above? Could his steadfast belief in a Celestial Heaven have anything to do with his intimate experience with desert heavens?

I cannot guarantee that my suppositions are true. But on the strength of this star-blessed evening in the Cabeza Prieta I can assert that, by day and by night, Arizona's deserts remain a part of "God's country" for those whose spirits are attuned to the firmament and what it declares.

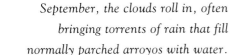

(OPPOSITE PAGE) *From the 9,000-foot heights of the Santa Catalina Mountains near Tucson, snowmelt cascades through Sabino Canyon to the thirsty desert below.*
RANDY A. PRENTICE

(FOLLOWING PANEL, PAGES 88-89) *A summer thunderstorm chases the sunlight in the Tucson Mountains, signifying the beginning of Arizona's monsoon season. Nearly every afternoon from mid-July to early September, the clouds roll in, often bringing torrents of rain that fill normally parched arroyos with water.*
BRUCE GRIFFIN

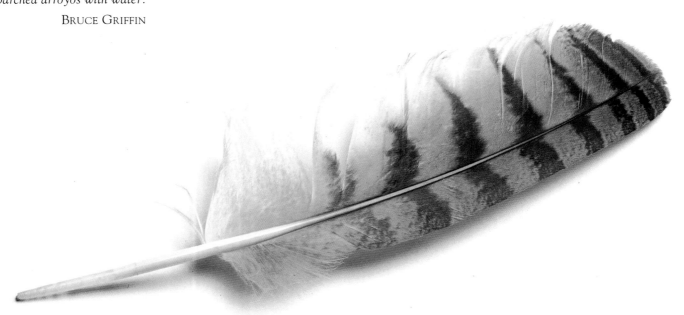

(ABOVE) *The saguaro provides both food and shelter to a wide array of birds, including the Gila woodpecker.*
SUZAN VICTORIA

(RIGHT) *Arizona's state bird, the cactus wren, occasionally nests in a hole made by the Gila woodpecker.*
C. ALLAN MORGAN

(BELOW) *The world's smallest owl is the elf owl, who also finds a woodpecker hole to its liking.*
SUZAN VICTORIA

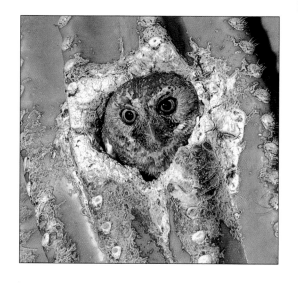

(FOLLOWING PANEL, PAGES 92-93) *A confident rock squirrel flips dirt with its nose to ward off a Sonoran gopher snake. Considering the size of the squirrel, the largest in its range, the snake may have felt it was a little more than it could swallow. Both animals survived the encounter.*
H. KNICKERBOCKER

9
1

92

(**LEFT**) *From the limbs of a dormant tree, this handsome bald eagle exhibits defiance. Until the white plumage appears on its head at about four years of age, an immature bird may be mistaken for a golden eagle or large hawk.*
ROGER WEBER

9
5

(**ABOVE**) *Belying its normally cuddly appearance, this coati displays formidable weapons. Unlike its cousin the raccoon, it does not have a black mask and prefers an arid open habitat.*
PAUL A. BERQUIST

(**FOLLOWING PANEL, PAGES 96-97**) *This coyote peers between bunchgrass and a prickly pear cactus while foraging in the desert. Present in Arizona since the Pleistocene epoch, its genius for survival compels admiration.*
PAUL A. & SHIRLEY BERQUIST

96

(LEFT) *Literally out on a limb, this ringtail breaks from its proclivity as a nocturnal animal and remains out in early dawn light. It is a relative of the raccoon and coati family. Curious little wide-eyed creatures, they have been known to steal into camp after the fire has gone out and rustle trail mix out of careless hikers' backpacks.*
ROBERT CAMPBELL

(ABOVE) *The sharp eyes of this Harris' hawk and the frailties of a Harris' antelope squirrel bring a wildlife drama to its conclusion atop a saguaro cactus. The Harris' hawk has a penchant for returning to the same perch day after day.*
DAN FISCHER

1
0
1

(FOLLOWING PANEL, PAGES 102-103) *The great horned owl, perched here in Antelope Canyon on the Navajo Indian Reservation, is the largest of the common owls and a skilled hunter of rabbits, rodents, skunks, and even other owls.*
JOHN MACMURRAY

(ABOVE) *The desert tortoise was once a supplement to the cuisine of Arizona's desert Indians. It has now been protected on the Sonoran Desert and classified as an threatened species on the Mojave Desert. Though ponderous, it can dig horizontal tunnels 30 feet long with its powerful forelegs.*

KEVIN K. HARRIS

(BELOW)*The Gila monster is usually slow and unaggressive. Depending on its body temperature, however, it is capable of considerable speed when threatened. If cornered it will hiss and display its teeth. Unlike a snake, the Gila monster does not strike. It clamps on and grinds its prey, transferring a very potent neurotoxic venom via grooved teeth. At up to 20 inches long, the Gila monster is the smaller of only two poisonous lizards in the world; the other is the beaded lizard of Mexico.*

SUZAN VICTORIA

(ABOVE) *Standing in a "garden" of its favorite food, prickly pear cactus, a collared peccary sniffs the air for danger. Though equipped with poor eyesight, it has a keen sense of smell. Vegetation changes over the past century have favored the species, and it is on the increase. Peccaries have a scent gland on their lower back for marking their territory and 2-inch-long canine teeth.*
PAUL A. BERQUIST

(FOLLOWING PANEL, PAGES 106–107)
Color-keyed to its habitat at Saguaro National Monument, this desert mule deer buck could be overlooked by the casual observer. Finding deer in cactus country regularly surprises visitors to the monument.
C. ALLAN MORGAN

108

(LEFT) *Leading interconnected lives, a giant saguaro cactus and paloverde tree grow adjacent to one another. The latter is often a "nurse tree" for the saguaro, providing shade from the scorching desert sun, and giving the saguaro's seeds a better chance for germination. Saguaro cactus regularly grow to 30 feet, may have dozens of arms, and can live as long as 200 years.*
DAVID MUENCH

1 0 9

(ABOVE) *Silhouetted against the Sonoran Desert sky, a Harris' hawk wings from the carcass of a saguaro cactus. Even in death the saguaro continues to be of use, harboring insects and small animals. The Harris' hawk, like other raptors, picks perches that allow expansive views of its domain.*
CHARLES BUSBY

(RIGHT) *Long-nose bats winter in Mexico, arriving in southern Arizona about the time the saguaros flower. Unlike most bats, which eat insects, long-noses feed upon nectar. They have a long, bristly tongue that may extend a quarter the length of their body.*
MERLIN D. TUTTLE,
BAT CONSERVATION INTERNATIONAL

(ABOVE) *The kit fox is nocturnal, shy, and rarely seen in the wild. It has feline-like features and movements, and a personality that is best described as "crafty." Reaching a mature weight of just 4 to 6 pounds, this tiniest of foxes is highly entertaining to those lucky enough to spot one.*
ROBERT CAMPBELL

(LEFT) *This coyote is dressed in its thick winter coat. With the ground blanketed in snow and many of its traditional food sources in hibernation, the coyote must cover much more terrain to find sufficient food. Many early-day explorers failed to distinguish the coyote from the wolf. Even today, it is often referred to as the "little prairie wolf."*
ROBERT CAMPBELL

Wet

From high in the dusky sky comes a call: *Ur-lank! Ur-lank! Ur-lank!* Unaware they are being watched, the wild geese spiral down, set wing, and splash to a landing on the green lagoon. Tired from their long migration, they paddle slowly to a small island where, as night falls, they file into a dense thicket of bulrushes and tules. Canada geese have returned to the Imperial National Wildlife Refuge. Here in this slender wilderness where earth meets sky and desert meets marsh, they will spend the winter until the tug of lengthening days pulls them north again.

Dawn breaks.

From above, the river resembles a meandering moat knifing through jagged, khaki-colored mountains. The lower Colorado is the southern terminus of a great funnel-shaped flyway that extends north to Alaska, and, behind screens of tall cattails, thousands of ducks and geese loaf on backwater lakes and hidden sloughs. A great blue heron gingerly high-steps along the river's edge, its beak a ready lance for unwary frogs or fish. In midstream, eight white pelicans dawdle on a sandbar, their brilliant plumage glinting with sunlight. A nearby mudflat is traced with a multitude of tracks, signing the presence of skunk, raccoon, beaver, and desert mule deer.

Lands

Upstream and down, this river has seen many changes, but here in this refuge, an ancient — and remarkable — way of life continues. Geese in the desert! Pelicans in the desert! Herons in the desert! Yes, water is indeed a great magician. The English poet Gerard Manley Hopkins said it this way:

What would the world be, once bereft
of wet and of wildness? Let them be left,
Oh let them be left, wildness and wet;
long live the weeds and the wilderness yet.

1
1
5

(LEFT) *Just like a conventional airplane, the American coot taxies for takeoff. Any observer of this water bird learns quickly where the expression "crazy as a coot" originated. Hunters show disdain for the "mud-hen," as it is sometimes called, because of its poor quality as table fare.*
JAMES TALLON

(FOLLOWING PANEL, PAGES 116-117) *Tamed by dams, portions of the lower Colorado River have spread out to create sloughs, marshlands, and back-bays that locals refer to as lakes. Numerous wildlife species find food and refuge here. Included among them are beaver, muskrats, and thousands of waterfowl, such as great blue herons, snowy egrets, Canada geese, and many species of ducks.*
MICHAEL COLLIER

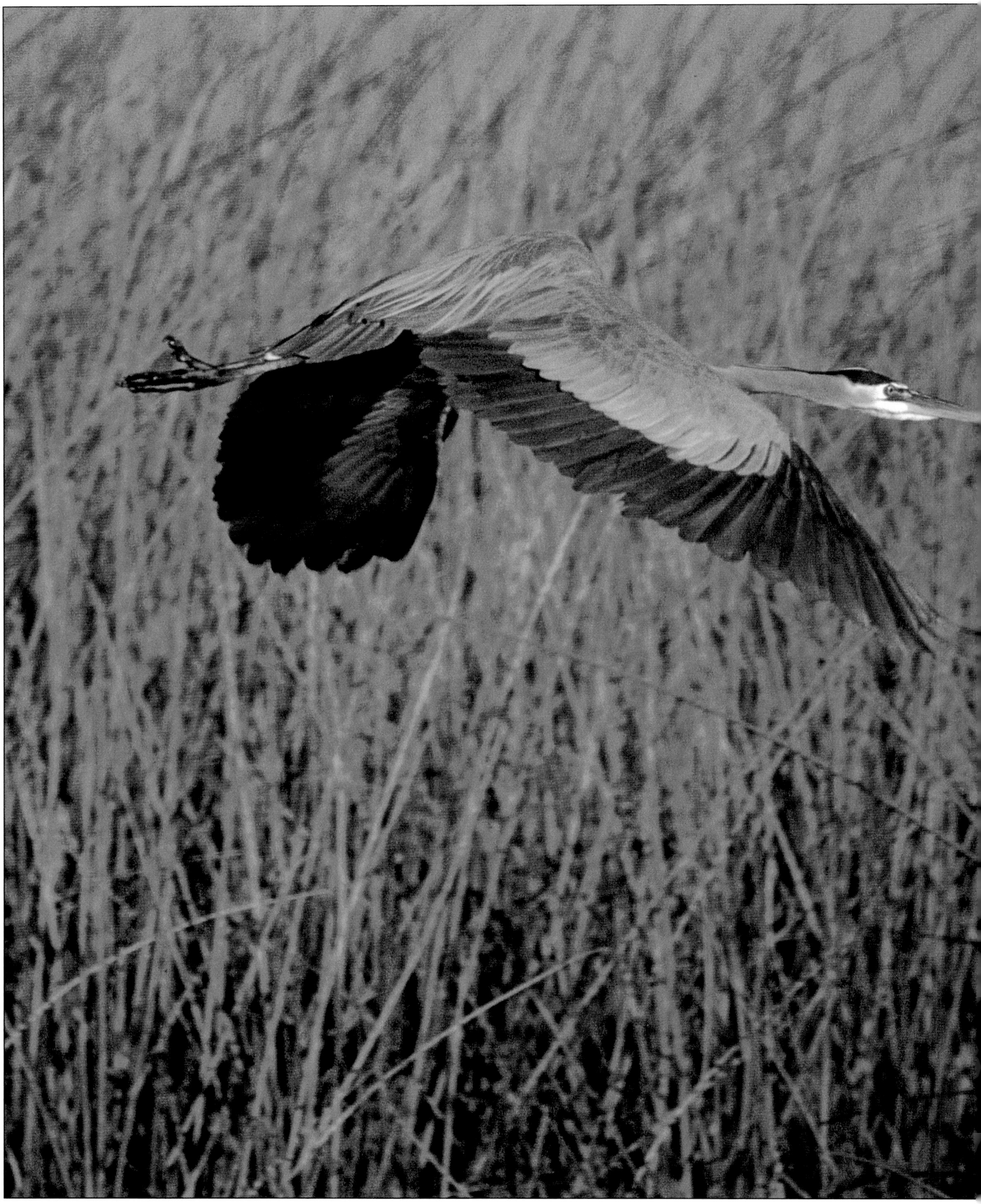

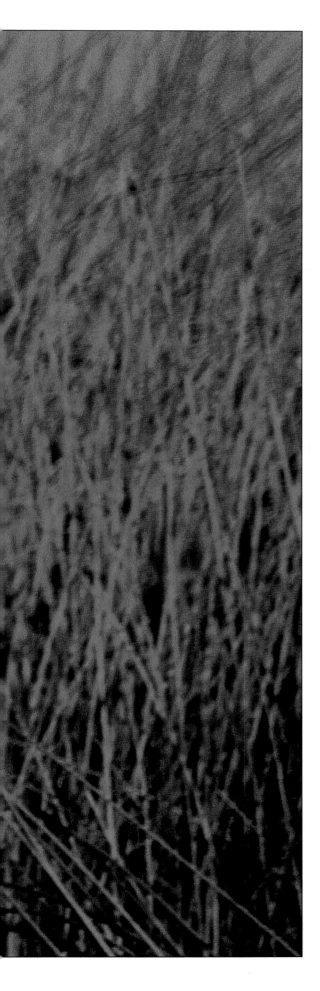

(LEFT) *A great blue heron skims the marsh grasses at Martinez Lake. It stands between 4 and 5 feet tall and has a wingspan of nearly 6 feet. One of many kinds of herons, the great blue stalks the shallow waters for fish, frogs, and other small aquatic animals.*
PETER ENSENBERGER

(ABOVE) *Buoyant and on an even keel, the American coot will tip its head up, duck-like, when feeding and, when necessary, dive like a grebe. Though only one-sixth the weight of a white pelican, the American coot must run even farther on the surface to get airborne. Gregarious and noisy, they frequently squabble among themselves without apparent reason.*
PETER ENSENBERGER

(ABOVE) *Perhaps just enjoying the sunshine, a member of the order Odonata, which includes about 400 species of dragonflies and damselflies, clings to a marshland reed. It spends most of its time in the air, feeding on small insects. From nymph to adult, its predaceous disposition helps control mosquitoes, midges, and other small insects.*
GILL C. KENNY

(FOLLOWING PANEL, PAGES 122-123) *No, it is not a source of warts. The*
Colorado River toad still earns amphibian celebrity status as the largest
Western species of toad, at up to 7.5 inches long. More smooth-skinned
than most toads, it secretes a toxin through its skin and a poison from
glands behind its eyes that are dangerous to dogs and other animals.
PAUL A. BERQUIST

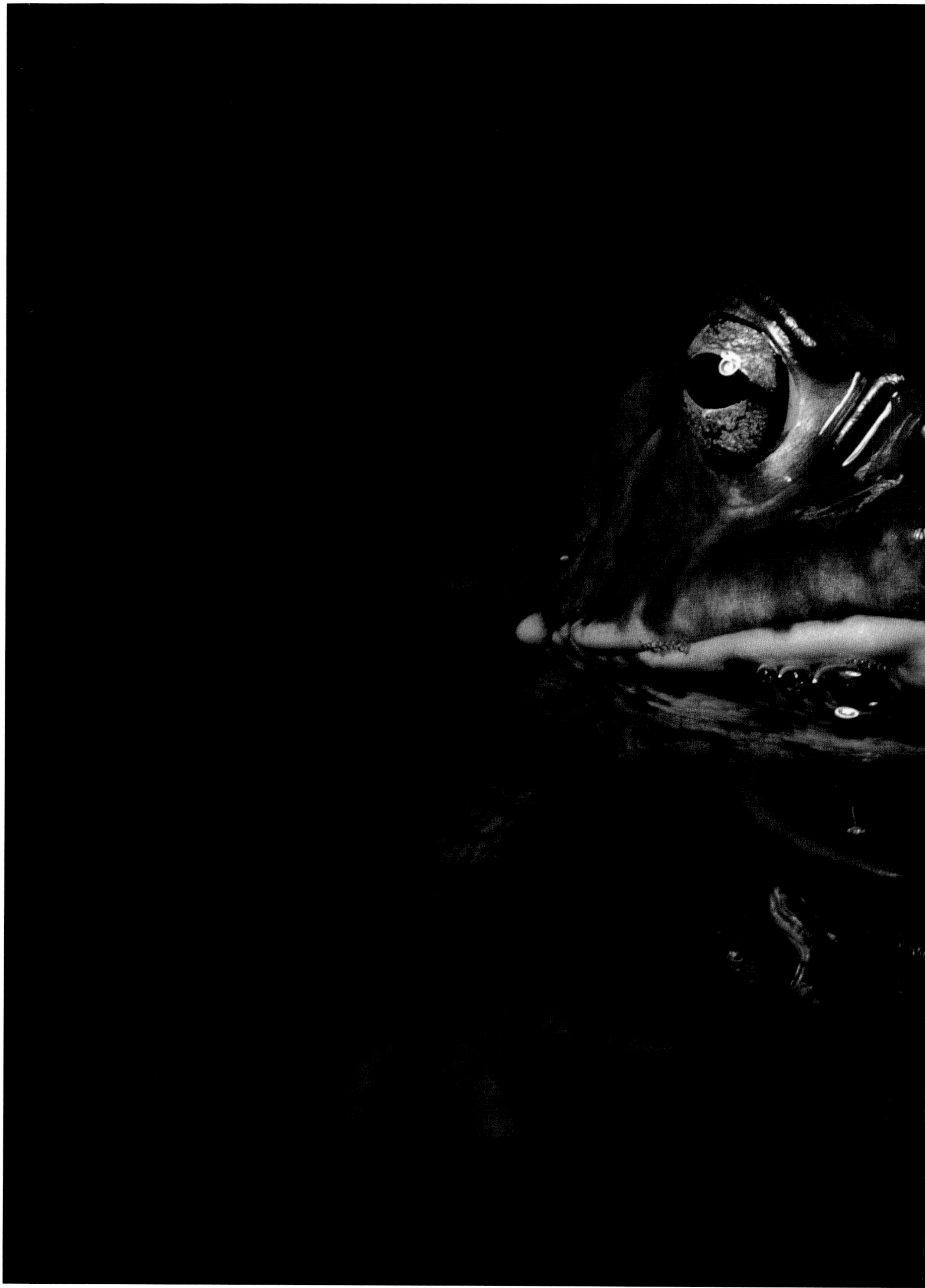

1
2
4

(LEFT) *Though smaller than the great egret, the snowy egret is equally elegant. Because of nuptial plumes that develop during the breeding season, snowy egrets became a prime target of the millinery trade in the early 1900s. Public outcry and pressure from Audubon groups led to their protection, and the showy, snowy egret has returned in abundance.*
PETER ENSENBERGER

(ABOVE) *Like other Canadian residents, the redhead winters in Arizona. Drainage, drought, and agricultural encroachment have destroyed about 80 percent of the redhead's historical habitat in the U.S. The redhead is a "pochard," defined as a diving duck. Its legs are set far to the back and wide apart, a design that is excellent for paddling, but awkward for walking.*
PETER ENSENBERGER

(BELOW) *Demonstrating a knowledge of aerodynamics, this osprey is carrying the fish headfirst — toward the direction in which it flies. Thought to be exclusively a fish-eater, the osprey dives from 100-foot heights, sometimes going completely beneath the surface of the water. It has unique talons that lock onto its catch.*
ROBERT CAMPBELL

(RIGHT) *Often in flocks of thousands, yellow-headed blackbirds dominate the sky at Cibola and Imperial national wildlife refuges on the lower Colorado River. Though not classed as a water bird, and often found in farmland and around grain fields, it prefers freshwater marshes and reedy lakes.*
PETER ENSENBERGER

(FOLLOWING PANEL, PAGES 128-129) *Popular with canoeists, Topock Gorge in Havasu National Wildlife Refuge rates as a top sanctuary for wildlife. Major waterfowl species include great blue herons, great and snowy egrets, double-crested cormorants, and numerous ducks and shorebirds. Coyotes sometimes are spotted standing in the shallows, and desert bighorn sheep skillfully negotiate "The Needles," the jagged riverside peaks.*
PETER KRESAN

129

(ABOVE) *Matching the color of its fall habitat, this American bittern, kin to the black-crowned night-heron, patrols the high-water shoreline for breakfast. When alarmed, the bittern often points its bill skyward, freezes, and blends into the brushy background.* JAMES TALLON

(BELOW) *On a sand bar in the lower Colorado River, a flock of American white pelicans rests prior to the late afternoon flight to feeding waters. Breeding birds have been reported flying 150 miles from their nests to feed. Unlike its smaller brethren the brown pelican, which dives from great heights to fish, the white dips its bill in the water for food while swimming.*
PETER ENSENBERGER

132

(ABOVE) *Intimidated by the sounds of an outboard motor, this great egret takes flight. It forages for meals of fish or frogs and even small snakes. Few other waterbirds equal its stealth. Like other egrets, its populations in America were decimated by plume hunters before it received protected status.*
PETER ENSENBERGER

133

(BELOW) *On a Colorado River backwater, Northern shoveler drakes make rounds for rations. Compared to speedsters like the canvasback, whose speed in flight can exceed 70 miles per hour, the shoveler is slow. Still, it makes swift and graceful takeoffs and landings and may come from as far as the Bering Sea to winter in Arizona.*
JAMES TALLON

1
3
5

(LEFT) *At 60 pounds, the beaver is North America's largest rodent. Far from the northern climes with which it is generally associated, the beaver is firmly established along the lower Colorado River. At Mittry Lake, where trees are sparse or non-existent, their lodges are constructed of mud.*
JAMES TALLON

(FOLLOWING PANEL, PAGES 136-137) *There are many backwater sloughs on the lower Colorado River that provide habitats for fish and wildlife and recreation for anglers, birders, boaters, and other outdoors folk. At the turn of the century, steamboats shuttled passengers and cargo past here to gold-, silver-, and copper-ore mining operations.*
JACK DYKINGA

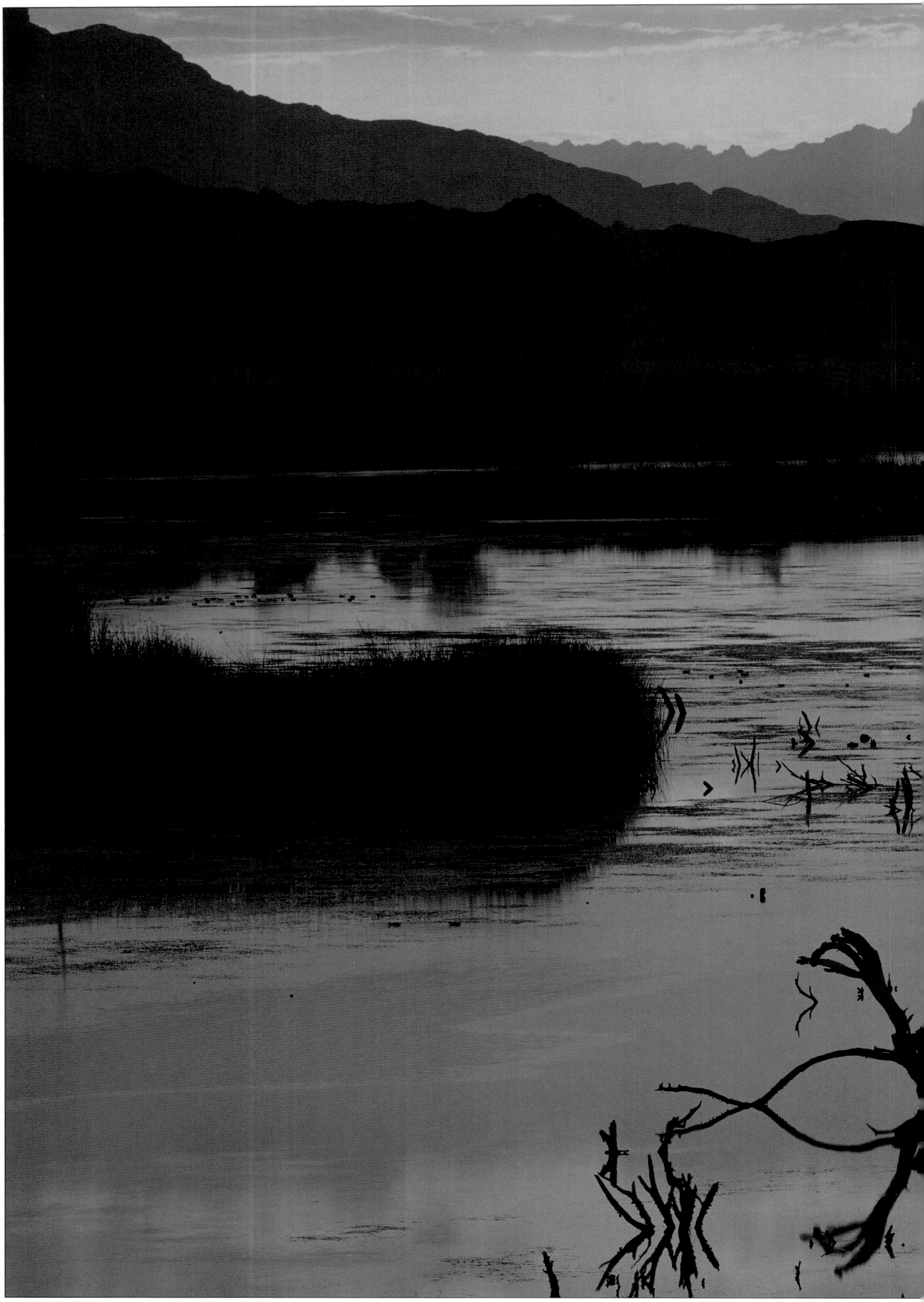

Epilogue

Hiding from the searing sun under a piñon tree 2,000 feet above the Colorado River, I rebuke myself for being so stupid. I should have known better than to try to hike out of the Grand Canyon on an abandoned mining trail in midsummer. And yet here I am — with my grandson Kyle Townsend in tow — wondering if my legs will get me to the South Rim by dark.

But I'm getting ahead of my story. Some months earlier, Grand Canyon Trust, an environmental organization, had asked me to host a week-long trip down the Colorado River for its members. Since I sit on the organization's board, I happily accepted the invitation, but on the condition that I could bring Kyle. A last-minute change in plans, however, made it impossible for me to spend an entire week on the river. In hindsight it would have been wiser to cancel. But, not wanting to disappoint Kyle, or the people from the Trust, I told them we would come for part of the trip.

And so, three days before, our small party of adventurers had hiked down the Bright Angel Trail to Phantom Ranch where we met the rest of the group and embarked on the river. Kyle was the youngest participant and I was the oldest. The head boatman put us in the bow of his oar-powered raft where he could keep a watchful eye on us as we bucked through Horn Creek, Granite, and Hermit rapids. It had been 24 years since I had been on the Colorado and this was Kyle's introduction to river running, but both of us reveled in the whitewater. The next day we ran the big one — Crystal —

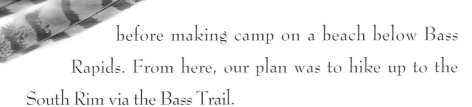

before making camp on a beach below Bass Rapids. From here, our plan was to hike up to the South Rim via the Bass Trail.

Having had a taste of the Canyon's fiery heat, I was apprehensive about what the morrow might bring, and that night, after Kyle went to bed, I had a chat with our boatman. He, too, was worried. Walking into the Grand Canyon is one thing; walking out on one of the hottest days of summer is another. This would be a challenging climb for someone in their prime. Though wiry for his age, Kyle was just 9 — and I was 71. Were we up to it? Once we left the river, there could be no turning back. The only thing that made our plan feasible was that the Trust had sent one of its interns down the trail to cache water at two spots. He and an outdoorswoman who had run the upper part of the river would accompany us back out. Having two sturdy guides and water in place would make a big difference, I reassured myself.

The next morning, we rose before dawn. After a hurried breakfast in the dark, our boatman rowed the hiking party across to the trailhead. By sunup we were moving. The

(LEFT) *Found from the sandstone reaches of the Navajo Indian Reservation to lava-country wilderness in Cabeza Prieta National Wildlife Refuge, the collared lizard seems entirely comfortable with its surroundings. Alert and agile, it is an excellent runner and jumper. It even catches and eats other lizards. The collared is considered amongst the most colorful of lizards.*
PAUL A. BERQUIST

first mile, in the coolness before the sun breasted the rim, was easy. When we reached the top of the Inner Gorge, we could see the jade-green river and our campsite far below. Kyle shouted and waved to the small, stick-like figures on the sandbar. Then, after saying goodbye to the boatman who had accompanied us this far, the four of us turned our attention upward. The real work lay ahead.

A long-abandoned mining trail that leaves the Rim 20 miles west of Grand Canyon Village, the Bass Trail is rarely hiked. Winding through a wild reach of the Canyon, the unsigned path descends 4,400 vertical feet in eight miles. My companions put Kyle out front and let him set the pace. They also gave him the responsibility of picking out the rock cairns that mark the winding trail where it has been obliterated by rains and rockfall.

We made good time for the first hour or two, but then, as the heat began to build, my pace slowed. Every few minutes, I found myself needing a breather. Between us, we were carrying two gallons of water. By 11 A.M., most of it was gone. When we reached the first water cache, we thankfully refilled our canteens and ate something in the shade of an overhang.

By now the temperature was approaching 110 degrees. No birds sang. Even the lizards and small creatures of the desert had vanished, seeking refuge in their burrows. After lunch, fatigued by the morning's exertions, I lay down on a rock and fell asleep. My nap ended when Kyle poked me in the ribs and said, "We've got to get going, Poppy." Thirty minutes later, switchbacking our way up the Redwall, we suddenly found ourselves boulder-hopping — we had lost the trail! Immediately I called a halt. We couldn't afford to waste energy or risk someone spraining an ankle. Sending our two companions back to relocate the trail, Kyle and I sought shade under a piñon tree, where I silently second-guessed my role in this risky venture.

"Are we going to make it out?" Kyle's voice interrupted my thoughts.

"We've got to," I said. "Have another drink. You've been setting a nice steady pace."

We sat there for a few minutes — grandfather and grandson — gazing out at the buttes and castles that rose shimmering out of the chasm. Our friends' shouts broke the silence. They had found the trail a few hundred feet above. We scrambled up to rejoin them.

The afternoon was a sun-baked grind, an agonizing test of a young boy's spirit and an old man's pride. Above the Redwall was a flat stretch across the Darwin Plateau and the last water cache. Then came the final thousand-foot climb. Kyle, showing no sign of his fatigue, stayed in front. My energies, though, were flagging, and I had to call for frequent panting stops. Slowly we inched skyward along the dusty trail.

And then, 10 hours after leaving the river, it was over. We were on the Rim.

"We made it, Poppy!" Kyle said, a note of triumph in his weary voice. I was proud of his spirit and stamina, and the praise that his newfound friends gave him seemed to make the whole ordeal worthwhile. "This is a hike you'll remember all your life," I said.

As I slumped, exhausted, into our vehicle, I wondered whether on this day I had passed the outdoor torch that my uncle had put in my hands in the White Mountains 60 years before.

(OPPOSITE PAGE) *From its treetop perch, this red-tailed hawk misses nothing. Hawks have the keenest vision known among animals, seeing more than eight times as much detail as do humans.*
JACK DYKINGA

(FOLLOWING PANEL, PAGES 142-143) *Geologists predict that over eons the Grand Canyon's magnificent rock formations will be constantly eroded by Nature's power tools — wind, rain, snow, and freezing and thawing — eventually becoming a broad valley.*
WILLARD CLAY

141

(ABOVE) *Standing on a saguaro, a Gambel's quail*
cock seems immune to the cactus' needle-sharp
spines. Like small roosters, the cocks seek high places
from which to "crow." Their plaintive "chi-ca-go"
call helps them to regroup. Quail nest on the ground.
To escape they prefer running to flying.
KEVIN K. HARRIS